I LOVE ISLAM

WORKBOOK

ISLAMIC STUDIES TEXTBOOK SERIES   **LEVEL 4**

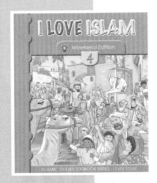

I Love Islam 4

Weekend Edition

I Love Islam © is a series of Islamic Studies textbooks that gradually introduces Muslim students to the essentials of their faith. It brings to light the historic and cultural aspects of Islam. This particular Weekend series covers levels one through six, which are suitable for young learners in part-time educational settings and includes student textbooks and workbooks as well as teacher's and parent's guides.

The Islamic Services Foundation is undertaking this project in collaboration with Brighter Horizons Academy in Dallas, Texas. Extensive efforts have been made to review the enclosed material. However, constructive suggestions and comments that would enrich the content of thiswork are welcome.

All praise is due to Allah (God), for providing us with the resources that have enabled us to complete the first part of this series. This is an ongoing project, and it is our sincere wish and hope that it will impact our Muslim children today, andfor many years to come.

Copyright © 2023 by Islamic Services Foundation

ISBN 1-933301-37-2

Printed in UAE

UNIT A

Exercise 1

Draw a picture.

In the box provided, draw a picture of the desert where Hajar and her son were left behind in.

Exercise 2

Matching.

Match the following Islamic terms with their correct definitions.

_____ 1. Hajar	A. Two landforms Hajar stood on to look for help.
_____ 2. Angel Jibreel	B. Isma'eel learned this by growing up in the Jurhum tribe.
_____ 3. Jurhum	C. A tribe visiting from Yemen.
_____ 4. Mt. Safa & Marwa	D. The elder son of Prophet Ibraheem.
_____ 5. Arabic	E. She was left along with her son in the desert.
_____ 6. Isma'eel	F. A supernatural being who with a hit on the ground brought water and relief to Hajar.

Exercise 3

Personal Questions.

1. What would you have done if you were in Isma'eel's place?

_____

_____

_____

2. Would you obey an elder if he told you that you must help build a building in the hot desert? What would you do? Write your answer then compare it with Isma'eel's.

_____

_____

_____

Exercise 4

Draw how the Ka'bah was built.

In the box below draw Al-Ka'bah as you think Prophets Ibraheem and Isma'eel built it the first time.

Exercise 5

Maze. As the Prophets Ibraheem and Isma'eel laid their very first stones they prayed to Allah.
Trace this maze and read the prayer.

Prayer: "Our Lord, accept this from us! You are the All-Hearing, the All-Seeing."

Exercise 1

Directions: Write two things a person must do when guests visit him/her, and at least one thing the guest should do.

1. _____

2. _____

3. _____

 ## Exercise 2

Maze.

Satan appeared and tried to stop Ibraheem from sacrificing his son. Find out which of these paths leads to the straight way, not to Satan.

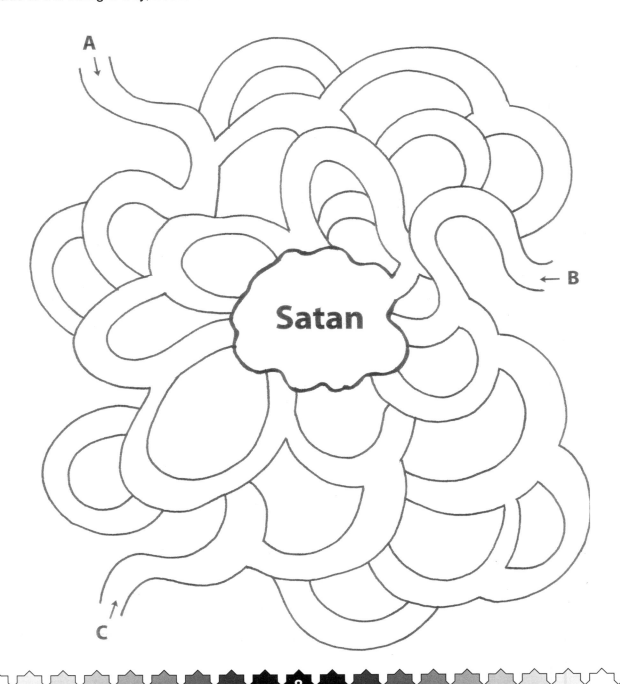

Exercise 3

Write the Hadeeth.

Below, write a hadeeth in Arabic and English that encourages the Muslim to be generous with his or her guests:

Arabic:

_____

_____

_____

English:

_____

_____

_____

Exercise 1

Draw a Map.

Draw the map of the Dead Sea as you see it in the Atlas or on page A24 of your textbook.

UNIT A
Chapter 3

Exercise 2

Fill in the blanks. (Refer back to the book on page A22.)

1. Allah sent Prophet _____ to the people in a small town called _____ near the Dead Sea.

2. He was the _____ of Prophet Ibraheem.

3. Prophet Lut called his people to _____ Allah.

4. The people of Lut disobeyed Allah and tried to _____ their Prophet.

5. One night Prophet Lut was visited by few _____.

6. Allah punished the disobedient people of Lut by _____ their village upside down.

7. There is a salty lake called _____ in the place where Prophet Lut and his people used to live. The lake is _____ miles long and _____ miles wide.

Exercise 1

Definition.

Define Hasad: _____

_____

Exercise 2

Good or Bad?

Help Noor decide which jealousy is good and which jealousy is bad. Indicate if the following statements are good or bad Jealousy. Write G next to each statement that describes a good form of jealousy and B if the statement describes a bad form of jealousy.

_____ 1. To be jealous that her brother read the whole Qur'an.

_____ 2. To be jealous that her classmate got a new backpack.

_____ 3. To be jealous that her cousin got long black hair.

_____ 4. To be jealous that her friend received a higher grade.

_____ 5. To be jealous that her neighbor got new clothes.

_____ 6. To be jealous that her brother got a new Nintendo game.

_____ 7. To be jealous because her brother doesn't miss any prayer.

Exercise 3

True or False?

Indicate if the following statements are true or false. Write next to the statements below (T) if the statement is true and write (F) if the statement is false:

_____ 1. Prophet Ya'qoob had four wives.

_____ 2. Yousuf was a righteous child, but not handsome.

_____ 3. Yousuf's brothers were jealous of him because he was more handsome than them.

_____ 4. In Islam you should wish for you brother what you wish for yourself.

_____ 5. Yousuf had a dream that he was pressing grapes to make wine.

_____ 6. Yousuf had ten brothers.

_____ 7. To make their evil plot look real, the brothers killed a goat to use its blood to stain Yousuf's shirt.

_____ 8. The father did not believe the story.

Exercise 4

Comprehension Questions.

List two things you learned from the story of Prophet Yousuf.

1.

_____

2.

_____

Exercise 1

You had no money, then suddenly Allah (swt) blesses you with money, what would you do with it?

Put a check in the box that describes a wise way to spend your money and write why in the lines below:

100 dollars:

☐ Spend all of it at once

☐ Spend a little of it at a time

20 dollars:

☐ Finish all of it

☐ Save some and use some

5 dollars:

☐ Use a little to have fun

☐ Use none to have fun

10 dollars:

☐ Use it on wasteful stuff

☐ Use it on useful resources

$100 _____

$20 _____

$5 _____

$10 _____

Exercise 2

Lying

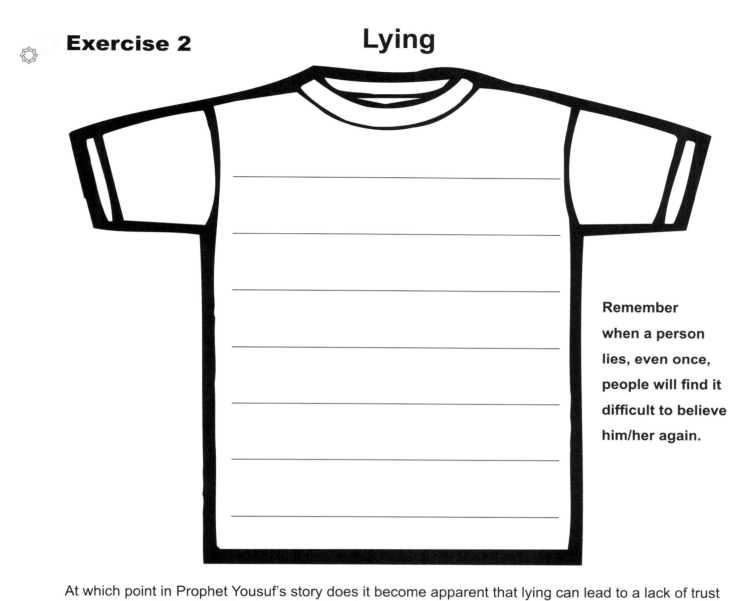

Remember when a person lies, even once, people will find it difficult to believe him/her again.

At which point in Prophet Yousuf's story does it become apparent that lying can lead to a lack of trust among others? On the shirt above describe the incident. Also on the lines
below, describe a similar incident that occurred in your life or someone else's life you may know.

_____

_____

_____

_____

Exercise 3

Factual Questions.

Answer the following questions:

1. How many brothers did Yousuf have?

_____

2. Why did Yousuf trick his brothers?

_____

3. What did the brothers use to cure their dad from blindness?

_____

4. How many skinny cows were in the king's dream?

_____

Exercise 4

Draw the skinny cows and color them as you wish.

Exercise 1

Right Hand and Left Hand.

Surat Al-Inshiqaq says something will happen to the people who will receive a book in their right hand or in their left hand. In the picture of the hands, write what will happen to them.

Left Hand

Right Hand

 **Exercise 2**

Matching.

Match the meaning with the right Arabic word:

Night	السماء انشقت
Painful punishment	الليل
Heaven bursts	القمر
Moon	يسجدون
Bow	عذاب أليم
Return	بيمينه
Man	مسرورا
Stretched	يحور
Earth	الأرض
Joyful	مدت
Right hand	الإنسان

UNIT B

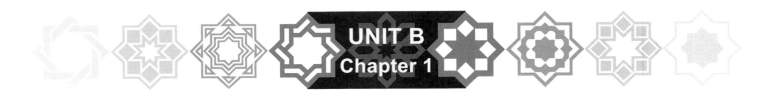
Exercise 1

Crossword.

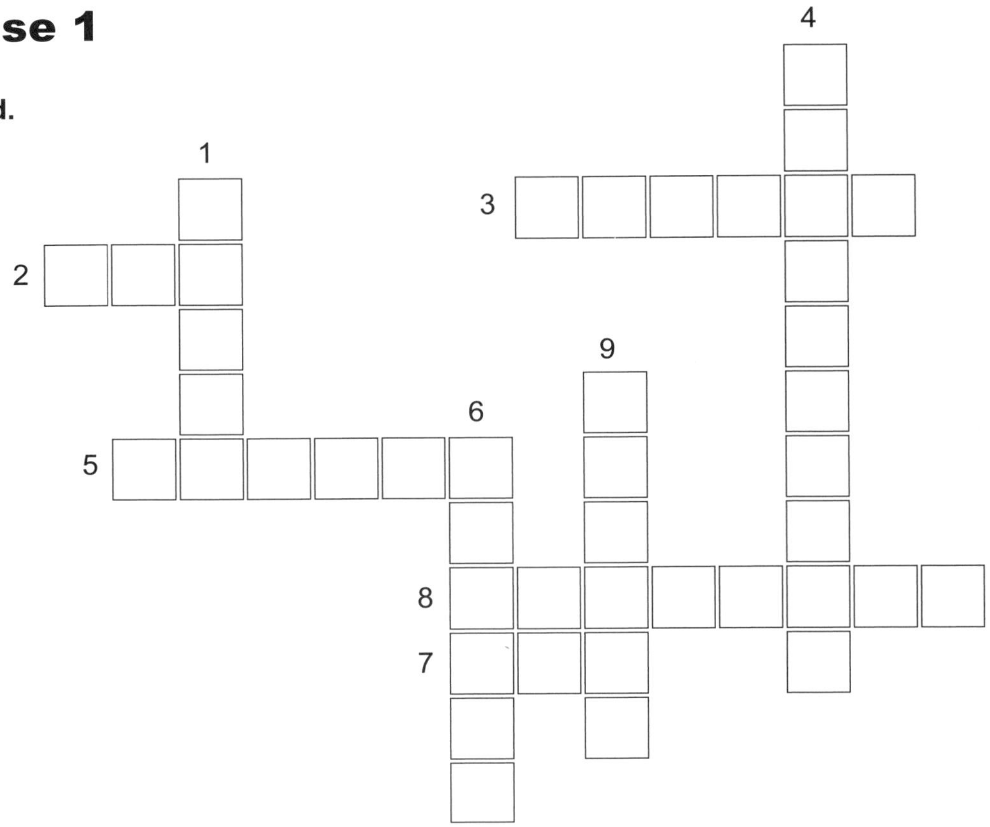

(crossword grid with numbered cells 1-9)

▶ Across:

2. The Prophet's cousin, _____, volunteered to lay in Prophet Muhammad's bed on the planned night, pretending to be the Prophet.

3. The leaders of _____, who were members of the Quraysh tribe, soon became tired of the Prophet.

5. They had tried throwing rocks and _____ at him.

7. There is only _____ God.

8. They were worried that Prophet Muhammad was challenging their _____.

▼ Down:

1. The Quraysh planned to murder the Prophet at _____

4. They offered him money and _____ if he'd stop teaching people about Islam.

6. Despite their bickering, the Prophet was _____ and patient.

9. Their plan was not successful and it _____ .

Exercise 2

Draw your answers. * Reminder: You should always love the Prophet more than yourself and anything in this world.

Draw five things that may get in the way of loving the Prophet, and then describe them in your own words.

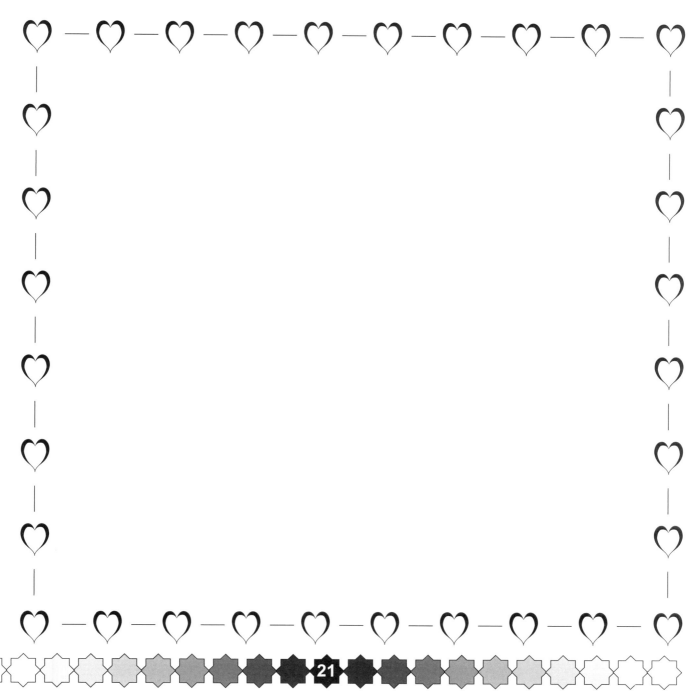

Exercise 3

In the box below, create a piece of art for Al-Muhaymin, one of the names of Allah, in Arabic and English.

Exercise 1

Comprehension Questions.

Throughout the Hijrah, the Prophet came upon two miracles. Next to the picture clue, describe the miracle and how it helped him and Abu-Bakr. For each miracle write a lesson you learned from it.

	Miracles	Lesson Learned

Exercise 2

Striving for Allah.

Even though sometimes it may be difficult to do something Allah loves, we should still do our best to obey Him. He will love us more and give us many Hasanat if we do so.

List how each of the following great people strived in the sake of Allah (swt).

1. Asmaa' bint abi Bakr:

_____

_____

2. Al-Muhajiroon:

_____

_____

3. Omar Ibn-Ul-Khattab:

_____

_____

List two things you can do for Allah's sake:

1.

_____

2.

_____

_____

Exercise 3

Write the du'aa'.

In the space below, write the du'aa' of travel in Arabic.

_____

_____

_____

Exercise 4

Write the nasheed.

Write the nasheed of Hijrah in Arabic in the space below.

_____

_____

_____

_____

_____

_____

_____

_____

Exercise 1

Matching.

Match the terms below with their correct descriptions.

_____ 1. Al-Ansar

_____ 2. Muhajiroon

_____ 3. The camel

_____ 4. Branches and leaves of date trees

_____ 5. The first Qiblah

_____ 6. Name of Prophet's mosque

A. People of Makkah who left to Madinahh.

B. They were used for the mosque's roof.

C. People of Madinah.

D. It chose the location of the mosque.

E. Al-masjid-un-Nabawi.

F. Al-masjid-ul-Aqsa in Jerusalem.

Exercise 2

Draw the Prophet's mosque.

In the box below, draw a picture of how the Prophet's mosque in Madinah looked when it was first built. Please note the following truths about its building:

- The Sahabah used bricks made from dirt.

- They created the walls from these bricks.

- The roof was made from the branches and leaves of date trees.

- Columns were made out of tree trunks.

- The ground was covered with sand and pebbles.

27

Exercise 3

First and second Qiblah.

Search for pictures of the first and second Qiblah. Cut and paste copies into the correct boxes below.

First Qiblah   **Second Qiblah**

Exercise 1

Draw the caravan.

In the box below, draw the caravan of Quraysh. Then on the lines below, explain why the Prophet wanted to capture the caravan.

```



```

Exercise 2

The Two Armies

Describe in the two circles below the Muslim army and the Quraysh army in the Battle of Badr.

Leader: _____

Number of Soldiers: _____

Faith: _____

Winner / Loser: _____

Leader: _____

Number of Soldiers: _____

Faith: _____

Winner / Loser: _____

Exercise 3

Draw your answers.

In the circles below, draw what you think made the Muslims win the Battle of Badr, then describe your answer in your own words.

Exercise 1

Battle Profile

Fill in the blanks to create a brief incident report on the battle discussed in Chapter 5.

Name of the Battle: _____

Time: _____

Place: _____

Fighting Parties:

       1. _____

       2. _____

Leader of Army 1: _____

Leader of Army 2: _____

Conclusions:

Who won the military battle?

_____

Exercise 2

Draw Jabal Uhud

Why do you think the Muslims did not win the Battle of Uhud? Draw Jabal Uhud in the box below, and then write your answer on it.

Exercise 1

Surat-ul-Ghashiyah 1-16

Write the number of the Arabic verse by the English translation:

___ And the Carpets spread out	هل أتاك حديث الغاشية (1)
___ In a lofty Garden	وجوه يومئذ خاشعة (2)
___ They have no food except thorns	عاملة ناصبة (3)
___ And drinking cups ready-made	تصلى نارا حامية (4)
___ Has the news of the great Hardship come to you	تسقى من عين آنية (5)
___ Going into burning fire	ليس لهم طعام إلا من ضريع (6)
___ And cushions set in a row	لا يسمن ولا يغني من جوع (7)
___ Well-pleased because of their deeds	وجوه يومئذ ناعمة (8)
___ Some faces on that day shall be gloomy	لسعيها راضية (9)
___ Therein are thrones raised high	في جنة عالية (10)
___ Which will neither fatten nor help against hunger	لا تسمع فيها لاغية (11)
___ Therein is a fountain flowing	فيها عين جارية (12)
___ Working hard and tired	فيها سرر مرفوعة (13)
___ Made to drink from a boiling spring	و أكواب موضوعة (14)
___ Other faces on that day shall be happy	و نمارق مصفوفة (15)
___ Wherein you shall not hear vain talk	وزرابي مبثوثة (16)

Exercise 2

Surat-ul-Ghashiyah 17-26

Fill in each blank with the English meaning of the Arabic word below.

Allah (swt) says about the disbelievers in ayat 17-26:

"Wouldn't they see how the _____ were created?"

الإِبِل

"And the _____, how it was raised high, and the _____, how they were

السـماء   الجـبال

firmly fixed, and the _____, how it was made a vast space?"

الأرض

UNIT C

Exercise 1

Comprehension Questions.

Define Rooh:

_____

_____

Inside each box below, draw what you think will happen to your body or soul if you skip good religious or physical activities.

Neglecting Body:

_____

_____

_____

_____

Neglecting Soul:

_____

_____

_____

_____

Exercise 2

Prayer is great food for your soul.

List five daily Fard prayers   List five healthy daily foods

1) How does food benefit your body?

_____

2) How does prayer benefit your soul?

_____

Exercise 3

Write the hadeeth.

What is the first thing a person will be asked about on the Day of Judgment? Answer this question with a hadeeth. Write the Arabic and English text in the spaces below.

Arabic:

_____

_____

English:

_____

_____

Exercise 1

Beware of Najasah

Fill in the blanks. Write some of the answers in Arabic and English.

The state of cleanliness and purity is called ___Arabic___|___English___. We must be in the state of

tahara when we ___Arabic___|___English___. When we are in the state of purity, we are

___Arabic___|___English___, or pure. Najasah can make us impure if it comes on our _____

or _____. The word _____ means "impurity." The six things which are considered impure

or unclean are _____, _____, _____, _____, _____, and _____.

Exercise 2

Write the hadeeth.

Is it really bad to use the bathroom and not clean and purify yourself very well? Support your answer with a hadeeth. Write the Arabic and English text in the spaces below.

Arabic:

_____

_____

English:

_____

_____

Exercise 3

Najasah and Tahara

Write an "N" next to the things which would make your body or clothes impure, and write a "T" next to the things in which you would still be tahir.

____ 1.If you are playing with your dog and you got dog saliva on you.

____ 2.If you had wudoo' but then you went and ate dinner.

____ 3. If you spilled soda all over your clothes.

____ 4. If you used the bathroom after making wudoo'.

____ 5. If you touched a pig and it licked you.

____ 6. If your cat licked your hand and face.

____ 7. If you held a dead animal.

____ 8. If you played with sand and rocks.

____ 9. If you vomited and it touched your body and clothes.

____ 10. If a car driving in the street on a rainy day splashed some water on you.

Exercise 1

Fill in the table.

Prayer	No. of rak'at of Fard	No. of rak'at of Sunnah
Fajr		
Thuhr		
Asr		
Maghrib		
Isha'		

Exercise 2

Fill in the blanks.

In the hadeeth below, fill in the missing words:

The _____ (s) said that "whoever prays _____ rak'aat of _____ prayer

during the _____ or _____ will have a _____ built for him in

_____ "

Exercise 1

True or False?

Indicate if the following statements are true or false, then correct the false statement on the line provided.

___1. Al-Jumu'ah means "the blessed day".

_____

___2. The best thing a muslim could do on Thursday is go to Friday prayer.

_____

___3. Reading Surat-al-Kahf is a very good thing to do on Fridays.

_____

___4. It is not good to talk during the khutbah, but you can whisper if you wish.

_____

Exercise 2

List 3 things a Muslim is recommended to do on Fridays.

1. _____

2. _____

3. _____

Exercise 3

Answer the following questions.

1. What was the story of the revelation of ayaat 9-11 of Surat-ul-Jumu'ah?

2. What is the hour on Friday where Allah will respond to whoever makes du'aa' to Him.

Exercise 4

Write a hadeeth.

Write a hadeeth in Arabic and in English on how special Friday is.

Arabic:

English:

Exercise 1

There are 8 things that invalidate your salah if you do them. What are they? Write your answers in the boxes below.

Exercise 2

Fill in the blanks.

1. When praying, boys and girls cannot show their _____.

2. If you _____ anything during salah, your prayer is broken.

3. If you purposely _____ an important part of the prayer, then your prayer is broken.

4. Most of the things that break prayer are not allowed because they will distract your

   _____.

5. Salah is not only a number of _____ movements, it is your _____

   connection with your _____.

Exercise 3

Write what the Prophet said when he saw a Sahabi looking around while he was praying.

_____

_____

_____

Exercise 1

Matching.

Match the words below to their meanings:

____1. النازعات   a. Blow (in the trumpet)

____2. زجرة   b. The day when Earth will shake

____3. قلوب   c. Angels who pull out the wicked soul

____4. واجفة   d. Shivering

____5. يوم ترجف الراجفة   e. Hearts

Exercise 2

Comprehension.

Summarize in your own words what happens in ayaat 15-26 of Surat-ul-Nazi'aat.

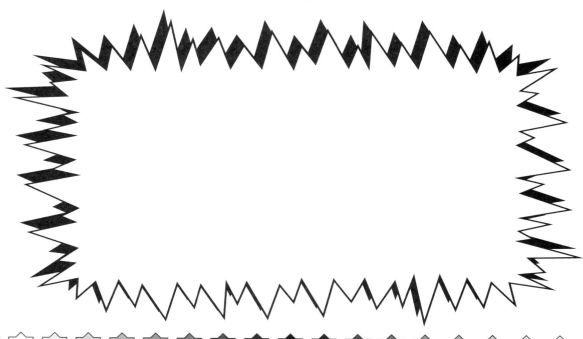

Exercise 3

Answer the following questions:

1. Which did Allah create first, the Earth or the heaven?

   _____

2. State the ayah in Arabic discussing the second creation.

   _____

3. The food that Allah made was for whom?

   _____

4. State that ayah in Arabic:

   _____

Exercise 4

Fill in the blanks.

1. The _____ ___ _____ is described in ayaat 34-41.

2. _____ will be for those who enjoyed dunya & forgot about the akhirah.

3. Allah will reward the one who stops himself from _____ with _____.

Exercise 5

In the two boxes below, draw pictures of how you imagine hell and heaven will look like.

Heaven	Hell

UNIT D

Exercise 1

Fill in the blanks.

Use the key terms in the box below to fill in the blanks below.

هجري	"new moon"	ميلادي	Omar bin Al-Khattab	هلال	moon	بدر

1. The Islamic calendar is based on the _____.

2. The solar calendar is called in Arabic "_____" calendar.

3. The lunar calendar is called in Arabic "_____" calendar.

4. The _____ marks the beginning year of the Islamic calendar.

5. _____ was the one who introduced the Islamic calendar.

6. When the moon is in a crescent shape it is called _____ in Arabic or _____.

7. The full moon is called _____ in Arabic.

Exercise 2

Write the ayah.

How many months are there in the lunar/Islamic year? Support your answer with an ayah, writing the Arabic text and its translation.

Answer:
_____

Ayah:
_____

Translation:
_____

Exercise 3

The Islamic Months

Fill in the crescents with the numbers and names of the months of the Islamic calendar in order.

Exercise 4

Write a five sentence paragraph explaining the importance of the month of Ramadan.

_____

_____

_____

_____

_____

Exercise 5

Write the hadeeth.

How many days are there in the lunar/Islamic month?

Answer: _____ or _____

Support your answer with a hadeeth, write the Arabic text and its translation:

Hadeeth:

_____

Translation:

_____

Exercise 1

What is Ramadan?

Decode the missing word to learn more about Ramadan.

A B C D E F G H I J K L M N O P Q R S T U V W X Y Z
26 25 24 23 22 21 20 19 18 17 16 15 14 13 12 11 10 9 8 7 6 5 4 3 2 1

Ramadan is the __ __ __ __ __ (NINTH) month of the Islamic calendar. It begins when
13 18 13 7 19

the __ __ __ (NEW) moon is sighted after the month of Sha'ban. Ramadan is also the
13 22 4

month of fasting, or __ __ __ __ __ (SIYAM). This means it is fard to fast during this month.
8 18 2 26 14

Siyam is a way of __ __ __ __ __ __ __ __ __ __ __ (WORSHIPPING) Allah by not eating or drinking from
4 12 9 8 19 18 11 11 18 13 20

__ __ __ __ (DAWN) to __ __ __ __ __ __ (SUNSET) each day . We also stay away from __ __ __ (BAD) deeds
23 26 4 13   8 6 13 8 22 7   25 26 23

and do extra __ __ __ __ (GOOD) deeds. Siyam teaches us to be __ __ __ __ __ __ __ (PATIENT) .
20 12 12 23   11 26 7 18 22 13 7

Muslims pray __ __ __ __ __-__ __-__ __ __ __ __ __ __ __ (SALAT-UT-TARAWEEH) every night in Ramadan.
8 26 15 26 7 6 7 7 26 9 26 4 22 22 19

One special night in Ramadan is __ __ __ __ __ __-__ __-__ __ __ __ (LAYLATUL-QADR), or the Night
15 26 2 15 26 7 6 15 10 26 23 9

of Power. This was the night the __ __ __ __ __ (QURAN) was revealed to the Prophet.
10 6 9 26 13

During this holy month, we are given the chance to gain lots of good deeds and

wipe away our __ __ __ __ (SINS).
8 18 13 8

Exercise 2   Ramadan

Draw your answer.

In the first box, draw how the moon should look when Ramadan begins. In the other box, draw how the sun will look when you break your fast.

Exercise 3

Things you do in Ramadan.

Draw four things you do with your family in Ramadan, and then write the benefit you get from each.

Exercise 4

Write the hadeeth.

Write a hadeeth about the blessings we get in the month of Ramadan.

Arabic:

_____

_____

_____

_____

_____

Translation:

_____

_____

_____

_____

_____

Exercise 1

True or False about fasting in Ramadan

Indicate if the following statements are True or False, and then correct the false statement.

___ 1. You break your fast at Maghrib, when the sun rises.

_____

___ 2. The meal in which we break our fast is called suhoor.

_____

___ 3. You start fasting at dawn.

_____

___ 4. Before Fajr prayer we eat a meal called suhoor.

_____

___ 5. We must make our intentions to fast only one day in Ramadan.

_____

___ 6. We should make du'aa before iftar because Allah answers our prayers at that time.

_____

___ 7. In Ramadan we only fast from food and drink.

_____

___ 8. We shouldn't break our fast as soon as possible after Maghrib.

_____

___ 9. Suhoor is a blessed meal.

_____

___ 10. It is not the Sunnah of the Prophet to break our fast with dates.

_____

Exercise 2

Read the pictures.

Beside each of the following pictures, write how you believe it relates to what you have learned about Ramadan.

_____

_____

_____

_____

_____

_____

_____

_____

_____

_____

_____

_____

Exercise 3

Ramadan Daily Dozen.

Write in the following boys or girls figures the Ramadan Daily Dozen.

Appreciating Allah's Gifts

Exercise 4

The Prophet recommended that we should have our iftar meals without getting overly full. Fill out the pie chart with how the Prophet told us to eat, then color each third differently.

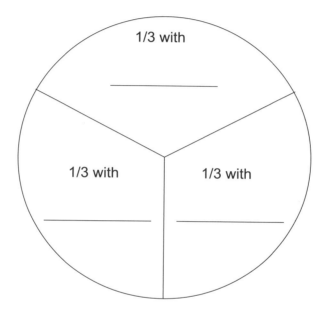

1/3 with

1/3 with

1/3 with

Exercise 4

Write the du'aa'.

Write the Du'aa you should say at iftar time.

Arabic:

_____

_____

Translation:

_____

_____

Exercise 6

Write the hadeeth.

Write a hadeeth about suhoor.

Arabic:

_____

_____

Translation:

_____

_____

_____

Exercise 1

Mona has a project in class to draw pictures of when it is okay to break your fast. Help her by drawing the pictures and describing why each breaks the fast.

Exercise 2

Do they break the fast?

Does each depiction offer a valid excuse to break your fast? Support your answers on the lines provided.

If you get
a little cut

_____

_____

If you
throw up

_____

_____

If you eat
by accident

_____

_____

If you're
traveling

_____

_____

If you go to
the restroom
and break your
wud'oo.

_____

_____

UNIT D
Chapter 5

Exercise 1

Circle the correct match for Salat-ut-Taraweeh and cross out the wrong ones. There is more than one possible answer for each.

Taraweeh:

1. Fard prayer

2. Prayer in the morning.

3. The Prophet encouraged us to pray it.

4. Sunnah prayer.

5. Prayed in Jama'ah

6. It's prayed in either eight or twenty rak'aat

7. Prayed two rak'aat at a time.

8. Means a "short review"

9. Can be prayed individually.

10. It's obligatory.

Exercise 2

In the moons below, write down four benefits of Taraweeh.

 ## Exercise 3

Q's & A's

1. What does "المزمل" Al-Muzzammil mean?

_____

2. The word Rattil, or "recite" in Suratul Muzzammil means.

_____

3. What is "رب المشرق والمغرب لا اله الا هو فاتخذه وكيلا" in English?

_____

Exercise 1

Write the three ways to study the Qur'an.

1 _____

2 _____

3 _____

Exercise 2

Content questions.

Answer the following questions of the story of Abu Dardaa.

1. Where was Abu Dardaa when the man came to him?

_____

2. Who was Abu Dardaa?

_____

3. Where did the man come from?

_____

4. Why did the man come to Madinah?

_____

5. What was in the hadeeth? Write three main points.

_____

Exercise 1

Fill in the blanks

1. Eid is on the 1st day of _____.

2. The _____ or crescent marks the end of _____.

3. Eid means _____.

4. _____ is prayed on Eid.

Exercise 2

Write 6 special things about Eid in the balloon.

1 _____

2 _____

3 _____

4 _____

5 _____

6 _____

Exercise 3

What is your favorite thing about Eid?

Exercise 4

Draw the shape of the moon that marks the end of Ramadan and the beginning of Shawwal.

Exercise 1

Lesson 1, Ayaat 1-5

Match each ayah (on the right) with its correct meaning:

a) And when the graves are dug out

b) And when the seas flow forth

c) When the heavens break apart

d) Every soul shall know what has done and what it has failed to do

e) And when the stars fall and scatter

___ ___ ___ 1) وإذا الكواكب انتثرت

___ ___ ___ 2) وإذا القبور بعثرت

___ ___ ___ 3) إذا السماء انفطرت

___ ___ ___ 4) وإذا البحار فجرت

___ ___ ___ 5) علمت نفس ما قدمت وأخرت

Exercise 2

Lesson 1, Ayaat 6-12

Write down the meaning of each word in English:

Word bank:

Form	Recorders	Human Beings	Guardian angels
Fooled you	Completed you	Disbelieve	Created you

5) صوت: _ _ _ _ _ _ _ _ _ _ _

6) تكذبون: _ _ _ _ _ _ _ _ _ _ _

7) لحافظين: _ _ _ _ _ _ _ _ _ _ _

8) كاتبين: _ _ _ _ _ _ _ _ _ _ _

1) الانسان: _ _ _ _ _ _ _ _ _ _ _

2) غرّك: _ _ _ _ _ _ _ _ _ _ _

3) خلقك: _ _ _ _ _ _ _ _ _ _ _

4) فسواك: _ _ _ _ _ _ _ _ _ _ _

Exercise 3

Lesson 1, Ayaat 13-19

Write three main lessons you learned from these ayaat:

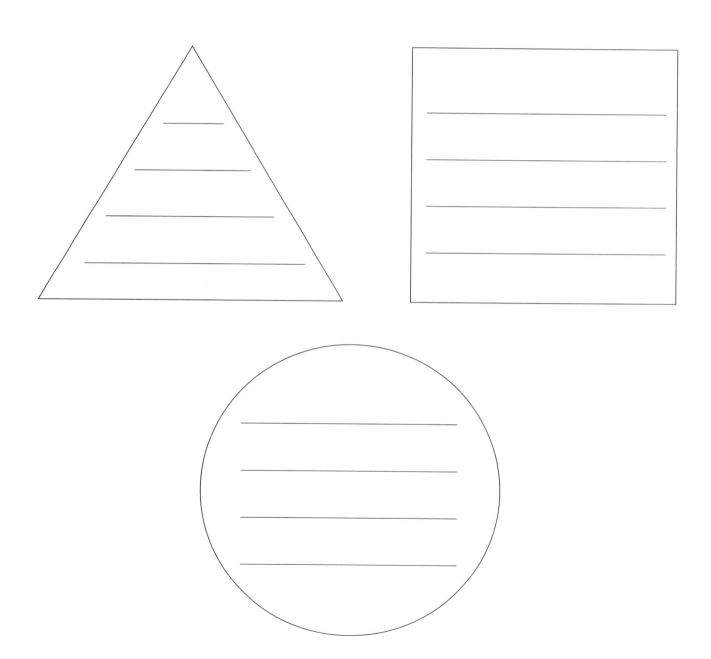

UNIT E

Exercise 1

Yes or No.

Next to each statement write "yes" if it is the right thing to do, and write "no" if it is the wrong thing to do.

_____ 1. Before going to sleep, kiss your parents goodnight and say "Assalamu Alaikum."

_____ 2. When you change into your pajamas, throw your clothes on the floor.

_____ 3. Before you sleep, recite your du'aa', Ayat-ul-Kursi and al-Mu'awwithaat.

_____ 4. Sleep on your right side.

_____ 5. Sleep on your stomach.

_____ 6. It is good to make wudoo' before sleeping.

_____ 7. When you hear the athan for Fajr, stuff your head under your pillow and go back
to sleep.

Exercise 2

Unscramble each underlined word to correctly complete each sentence.

Word bank:

Taharah	Ayat-ul-Kursi	Sunnah	An-Nas	Al-Falaq
	Al-Ikhlas	Day	Live	Fajr	

1. It is the Sunnah to make wudoo' before sleeping, and to sleep in the state of

   <u>hrahata</u> _____ (purity).

2. Before going to sleep recite:

   *Surat <u>la-salkhi</u> _____

   *Surat <u>al-laqaf</u> _____

   *Surat <u>na- san</u> _____

   *and ayat <u>lu-rsiuk</u> _____

... continue

Exercise 2 (continued)

3. We sleep on our right sides, because it is the <u>nnusha</u> _____ to do so.

4. When we wake up each morning, we should be happy that Allah has given us another

   <u>dya</u> _____ to <u>vlie</u> _____.

5. When it is time for <u>jfar</u> _____, we should wake up and pray instead of continuing

   our sleep.

Exercise 3

Du'aa' of sleeping.

Write down the du'aa you should say before sleeping.

Arabic:

_____

_____

_____

English:

_____

_____

_____

Exercise 4

Du'aa' of waking up.

Write the du'aa' you should say when you wake up.

Arabic:

_____

_____

_____

English:

_____

_____

_____

Exercise 1 — Surat-un-Naba'

In ayaat 1-16, Allah (swt) describes a few of the blessings He has sent for us. In the box, draw some of the things Allah has discussed in the ayaat, then explain what you drew.

Exercise 2

Circle the items below that relate to ayaat 17-30 in Surat-un-Naba'. Then discuss how they relate to the ayaat.

_____

_____

_____

_____

_____

_____

 **Exercise 1**

Surat-un –Naba' (Ayat 31-40)

Match the following Quranic terms with their correct meanings.

____ Gardens	A) رب السماوات
____ Cup	B) الروح
____ Pure	C) دهاقا
____ Dust	D) حدائق
____ Lord of the heavens	E) الرحمان
____ Warned you	F) مآبا
____ Day of Truth	G) كأسا
____ Spirit	H) أنذرناكم
____ Protection	I) اليوم الحق
____ Merciful	J) ترابا

Exercise 1

Manners of Eating

Fill in the blanks:

1. Before eating we should make sure we are neat and

2. Before we eat we should have a

3. If a certain food is out of our reach, we should

4. We should not eat the food if it is too hot. Instead, we should

5. While we are eating, we should remember to be

6. If we have a lot of food in front of us, we should

7. Below, draw two of your favorite foods then draw a haram food.

Favorite food	Haram food

Exercise 2

A) Du'aa' before eating.

Write down the du'aa' you should say when you start eating.

Arabic:

_____

_____

Translation:

_____

_____

B) Du'aa' after eating.

Write down the du'aa you should say when you finish eating.

Arabic:

_____

_____

Translation:

_____

_____

Exercise 3

In the box below, create a piece of art for Al-Muqeet, one of the names of Allah, in Arabic and English.

UNIT F

UNIT F
Chapter 1

Islam in Africa

Exercise 1

Fill in the blanks and find your answers in the puzzle.

A	K	Q	W	A	Z	Y	H	A	H	N	F	O
N	L	S	U	I	P	E	Q	X	B	O	P	M
N	M	U	M	R	R	C	N	Z	C	J	R	A
A	N	O	N	E	G	Y	P	T	Q	V	W	R
G	O	H	T	G	T	C	G	Y	S	F	V	P
A	S	U	W	L	O	M	I	U	L	I	J	M
S	O	K	B	A	H	I	B	N	N	A	F	I
H	N	A	M	R	O	T	X	I	M	E	G	E
I	U	R	B	A	F	R	I	C	A	D	H	O

1. Muslims fled and found protection under the Abyssian Christian king named _____

2. _____ spread Islam throughout North Africa.

3. _____ and Egypt are the largest Muslim African countries.

4. After Islam came to Makkah, _____ was the first land to learn about Islam.

5. _____ decided to invite the people of Egypt to Islam..

Exercise 1

Beautiful Mosques

In the boxes below, draw a small picture of the mosques you learned about. On the lines beside your picture, write an interesting fact you learned about it.

Mohammad Ali Mosque

Sidi Okbah Mosque

Yaama Mosque

Djenne Mosque

Exercise 2

African Mosques

In the first box draw an African masjid, and in the other box draw the masjid you usually go to. At the bottom, discuss the similarities and differences between them. Have fun coloring!

Exercise 1

The Nile River

On this side of the river write down some well-known places and things in Egypt.

On this side write some well-known attractions in Cairo.

Exercise 2

Egypt

In the pyramid, color the true facts green and the false facts red. On the side, correct each false statement.

The Nile River passes from south to north

Egypt became the first Muslim nation in Africa.

Salah-ud-Deen was one of the least important leaders of Egypt.

Al-Azhar University was founded in 970 AD and is one of Cairo's oldest mosques.

Egypt is well-known for its rivers and farms.

Muslims make-up 94% of Egypt's population.

Exercise 1

Write in the correct country to answer each of the questions below.

1. Which African country has the lowest percentage of Muslims?

_____

_____

_____

2. Which African county has the highest percentage of Muslims?

_____

_____

_____

3. How many countries are in North Africa?

_____

_____

_____

4. What is the capital city of Libya?

_____

_____

_____

5. Who was the leader who helped spread Islam in North Africa?

_____

_____

_____

UNIT F
Chapter 4

✿ **Exercise 2:** Word Search

Spread of Islam to North Africa

```
M  O  R  O  C  C  O  R  O  M  S  A  A  A  A  A  A  A  A  S
N  N  A  D  U  S  E  G  Y  P  T  Y  Y  Y  Y  Y  R  I  L  A
A  I  R  E  G  L  A  S  N  A  O  B  B  B  B  A  N  G  A  O
A  A  I  R  E  G  L  A  I  C  A  I  I  I  H  A  E  I  O  C
T  M  A  E  B  Y  D  S  C  I  L  L  L  A  T  O  S  C  L  H
P  O  I  G  N  U  I  O  R  T  O  A  S  I  C  I  C  C  I  P
Y  R  R  Y  S  N  R  E  A  C  I  N  R  C  N  O  L  I  B  A
G  O  E  P  U  O  G  Y  C  S  R  U  O  U  R  E  G  Y  P  T
E  C  G  T  M  L  B  O  I  E  A  R  T  O  C  C  O  R  O  M
M  C  L  A  A  I  R  N  T  M  O  I  M  B  U  A  Y  B  I  L
A  O  A  Y  L  O  U  S  N  M  O  R  O  C  C  O  R  O  M  C
U  R  Y  B  M  T  E  H  A  E  U  M  M  A  Y  Y  A  D  S  O
R  O  B  I  L  W  S  U  D  A  N  M  F  A  L  G  E  R  I  A
I  M  I  L  I  B  Y  A  U  S  U  M  M  A  Y  Y  A  D  S  G
T  A  L  G  E  R  I  A  S  E  S  U  D  A  N  E  G  Y  P  T
A  O  K  B  A  H  I  B  N  N  A  F  I  T  G  E  G  Y  P  T
N  U  M  M  A  Y  Y  A  D  S  A  A  A  A  I  S  I  N  U  T
I  M  O  R  O  C  C  O  R  O  M  O  R  O  C  C  O  R  O  M
A  A  N  U  M  M  A  Y  Y  A  D  S  U  D  A  E  G  Y  P  T
H  B  N  S  I  I  I  H  Y  A  I  B  F  A  C  T  M  N  I  L
```

Use the clue to figure out the word. Write the word and find the word in the word search puzzle.

1. A country who's capital city sounds almost the same as the country.

   Write the word: ⎯ ⎯ ⎯ ⎯ ⎯ ⎯ ⎯

   found _____ time(s) in the puzzle

2. The Islamic Dynasty that ruled Muslims in North Africa.

   Write the word: ⎯ ⎯ ⎯ ⎯ ⎯ ⎯ ⎯ ⎯ ⎯

   found _____ time(s) in the puzzle

3. A country who's total Muslim population is only 73%

   Write the word: ⎯ ⎯ ⎯ ⎯ ⎯ ⎯

   found _____ time(s) in the puzzle

4. 100% Muslim population in North Africa

   Write the word: ⎯ ⎯ ⎯ ⎯ ⎯ ⎯ ⎯ ⎯ ⎯ ⎯

   found _____ time(s) in the puzzle

5. The name of a desert, with not a very high population

   Write the word:

   ⎯ ⎯ ⎯ ⎯ ⎯ ⎯ ⎯ ⎯ ⎯ ⎯ ⎯ ⎯ ⎯ ⎯

   found _____ time(s) in the puzzle

6. The leader of the Dynasty that spread Islam to North Africa

7. The starting country in North Africa that spread Islam to the other countries

   Write the word: ⎯ ⎯ ⎯ ⎯ ⎯ ⎯ ⎯

   found _____ time(s) in the puzzle

8. Home of the Pyramids

   Write the word: ⎯ ⎯ ⎯ ⎯ ⎯ ⎯

   found _____ time(s) in the puzzle

9. A country in North Africa with a Muslim population of 97%

   Write the word: ⎯ ⎯ ⎯ ⎯ ⎯ ⎯

   found _____ time(s) in the puzzle

10. The smalles North African country.

    Write the word: ⎯ ⎯ ⎯ ⎯ ⎯ ⎯ ⎯ ⎯

    found _____ time(s) in the puzzle

Exercise 1: Nigeria

Use the box below to list some of the tribes of Nigeria listed in the book, and write down an interesting fact about each, such as language spoken, work, or other tribe information.

Nigerian Tribe	Interesting Fact

 ## Exercise 2

Unscramble the words listed below.

1. JAUAB: _____

2. BAUYRO: _____

3. OSGAL: _____

4. BOGL: _____

5. IANULFAAUSH: _____

6. IAREGIN: _____

7. CAARIF: _____

8. DANABI: _____

!!BONUS WORD!!

WUANLOOJMKEHEA

_____

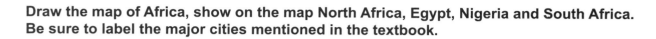

Exercise 1

Draw the map of Africa, show on the map North Africa, Egypt, Nigeria and South Africa. Be sure to label the major cities mentioned in the textbook.

Exercise 2

The statements in the boxes below represent a letter. Color in the statements that are true. After you have colored in all the statements that are true, solve the secret word by using the letters from the boxes you colored in.
Hint: The secret word has 11 letters!

A The capital of South Africa is Pretoria.	B South Africa is in Southern Africa	U Ahmed Deedat is from South Africa	F There are 1 million Muslims in S. Africa.
S The total population of South Africa is 44 million.	O Durban is a city In South Africa.	A There are 1 billion Muslims in S. Africa.	I Ahmed Deedat passed away in 2005.
R One masjid in South Africa is called Jummah Masjid.	H South Africa has a very involved Muslim community.	L Tripoli is the capital of South Africa.	Z South Africa has the most Muslims in all of Africa.
F South Africa has many nationalities that make up the country.	C Johannesburg is a major city in South Africa.	M The language of South Africa is called Africa.	T There is a masjid in South Africa called Gray Mosque.

Solve the word:

— — — — — — — — — — —

UNIT G

Exercise 1

Brotherhood in Islam

For each incident described below, write down what you would do and why.

1.
> You're eating a big meal and someone beside you is hungry, though you aren't full yet.

_____

_____

_____

2.
> You're resting and watching TV when your little sister asks for your help with her homework.

_____

_____

_____

3.
> You see the new student at your school all alone during recess time.

_____

_____

_____

4.
> You're playing soccer and you see a kid fall and get hurt.

_____

_____

_____

Exercise 2

Brotherhood in Islam

Write down in the box how the Prophet (peace be upon him) created brotherhood between Al-Muhajireen and Al-Ansar.

Now write what you have learned about brotherhood in Islam, and how you can use it in your life to become a better Muslim.

Exercise 1

Allah says that we should respect our parents, especially our mothers, since heaven (Jannah) is under the mother's feet.
Write a poem that you will give your mother, expressing your love and care towards her.
Draw a bouquet of flowers to go with your poem! Be creative!

Exercise 2

Right or Wrong

Answer each scenario by marking it either right or wrong.

1. Zayd did not like Ahmed very much, but since his mother pushed him to act nice, Zayd reluctantly was nice to him. _____

2. Aminah was hurt by her friend Ayah, but for the sake of Allah, she forgave Ayah and treated her nicely. _____

3. Nada and Reem did not like anyone that was not Muslim, and showed it by being rude. _____

Exercise 3

Write the hadeeth that expresses the importance of being kind to people. Please write it in both Arabic and English.

Arabic Text: _____

_____

_____

English Text: _____

_____

_____

Exercise 1

List the 6 rights of Muslims to fellow Muslims and give a personal example of how you have represented those 6 acts towards friends, families, or other people in your life.

1. _____

   _____

2. _____

   _____

3. _____

   _____

4. _____

   _____

5. _____

   _____

6. _____

   _____

Exercise 2

Right or Wrong: Answer each of the following by writing how you would react to the situation using the six rights of all Muslims to each other.

I'm new to the school and very nervous. I don't know anyone.

_____

_____

_____

_____

I am very sick, "Achoo!" I can't stop sneezing.

_____

_____

_____

_____

My mom had a terrible car accident and I had some injuries from it. It's very boring in the hospital alone.

_____

_____

_____

An Eid party would be fun. Come over to my house this Saturday.

_____

_____

_____

I'm having a really hard time with my new little brother at home. What can I do?

_____

_____

_____

My grandmother passed away. We have to pray for her at the masjid on Friday.

_____

_____

_____

_____

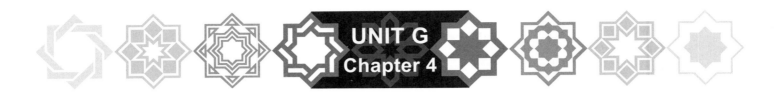

Exercise 1

Draw 4 different things that you would be able to give someone. After you have drawn the items, briefly write a description of each.

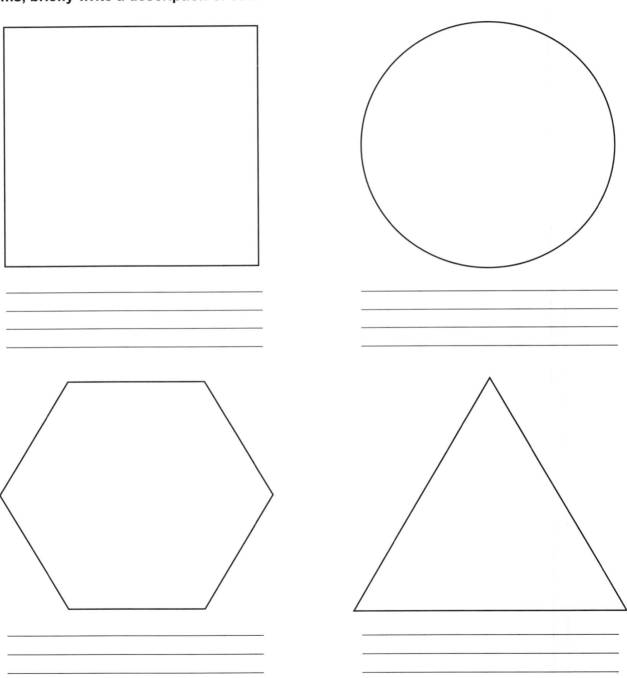

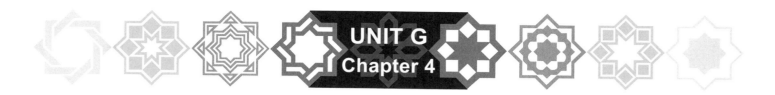

Exercise 2

Right or Wrong

Answer the following questions:

1. Why is giving charity important?

   _____

   _____

2. Have you ever given charity? If so, how did that make you feel?

   _____

   _____

3. What did the Prophet say about giving charity?

   _____

   _____

4. What type of charity should be given to the needy? List some examples.

   _____

   _____

5. Is smiling a form of charity? Answer why or why not.

   _____

   _____

Exercise 1

Answer each of the following as either Gheebah or Nameemah then explain why.

1. Nagi was jealous that Ali became friends with Ahmed, so Naji told Ahmed that Ali does not really like him, and is just using him.

_____

_____

2. Samia and Batool were out shopping when they saw their classmate Aisha. Samia whispered to Batool that Aisha's outfit was not very nice and they both started laughing.

_____

_____

3. Aminah and Ayah were really good friends until Ayah heard that Aminah was saying things about her to their mutual friends.

_____

_____

EXERCISE 2:

It seems like everyone has gossiped at least once in their lifetime. Some do not know the dangers of it. What if a friend of yours said something bad that hurt you? How would you respond?

_____

_____

_____

What are the dangers of Gheebah and Nameemah? How can they both be avoided?

_____

_____

Why is lying a sin?

_____

Exercise 2

Complete the crossword puzzle.

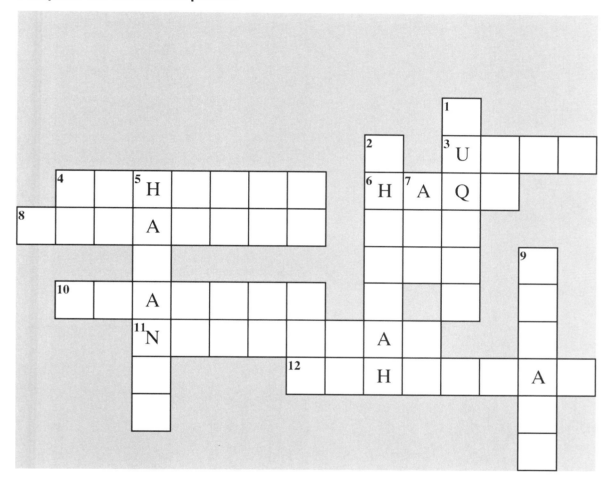

Across

3 Sister
4 Plural for sisters
6 Right in Islam
8 Arabic for hellfire
10 giving to the needy
11 Breaking up a relationship
12 Brotherhood

Down

1 Plural for Rights in Islam
2 Saying something bad about someone else
5 Good deeds
7 Brother
9 Questioning